SONGS SIGNS AND STORIES
by John Horton

Designed & Illustrated by Michael Kennedy

Pupil's Book One
ED 11409A

Schott & Co. Ltd, London
48 Great Marlborough Street
London W1V 2BN

B. Schott's Söhne, Mainz

Schott Music Corporation, New York

© 1985 Schott & Co. Ltd, London

ED 11409A

ISBN 0 901938 61 0

SOUNDS AS SIGNALS

Ambulances, fire engines, and police cars have a special signal to warn other traffic to give way to them. The signal has two different sounds, one higher than the other. The two sounds make a pattern like this:

These two sounds are usually just one step apart, and we can give them playing names which are letters of the alphabet, and also singing or solfa names:

A	B	A	B	A	B	A	B
ray	me	ray	me	ray	me	ray	me

If you have a descant recorder you can easily play this pattern. Practise singing it too.

Suppose a vehicle needed a signal that was different from an ambulance, fire engine, or police car. It might have a three-note pattern that went up and down by steps.

To show the steps clearly we have had to use two lines, one for the G and the other for the B, and A fits into the space between them:

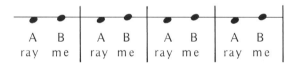

Playing names	G	A	B	A	G	A	B	A	G	A	B	A	G
Singing names	doh	ray	me	ray	doh	ray	me	ray	doh	ray	me	ray	doh

Play the three-note signal and sing it, and then find it on the piano. Here is a picture to help you.
[Notice the three black keys that stand close together, and then play a white key to the right of each black one.]

Playing names are the first seven letters of the alphabet: A B C D E F G. When they are all used up we start again.

Sound signals move up and down evenly and regularly. When we write out their patterns we can show that they are regular by fitting an upright stroke or 'stem' to each note:

(Our new 3-note signal)

A note with a black head and a stem attached to it is called a *crotchet*.

Things to do

1 Keep a diary of police car, fire engine, and ambulance signals that you hear, and try to write out their patterns. Notice that sometimes the signal begins with the top note of the pattern, and sometimes with the bottom one. Can you hear any difference between one vehicle and another?

2 Practise playing the 3 notes G A B on the recorder, the piano, and any other instruments you have.

3 Practise writing crotchets. Begin with the head, a neat oval shape, not too large:

Then fit on the upright stem, not too thick and not too long:

Sometimes the stem goes on the other way round:

4 If we have 3 different sounds, like G A B, there must be 1 x 2 x 3 ways of arranging them. (Work out that sum.) We have tried them in the order G A B and B A G. Find the other ways, play them and sing them, and then write them out, with a crotchet for each note. Of course you will need to draw two lines first (not too close, not too far apart).

5 Think of some more sounds that come in regular patterns. Here are a few:

> walking or running footsteps
> windscreen wipers
> dripping tap
> your own heart-beats

MORE ABOUT SIGNALLING WITH SOUNDS

Long ago men out hunting or fighting in groups found ways of signalling to one another. They blew into the horns of dead animals, or hollow wooden tubes, or large shells. These made sounds that were louder than shouting, and could be heard over great distances. When working in metal had been discovered, they were able to use horns and trumpets modelled in copper or bronze or iron which gave an even louder and clearer set of signals.

Most of these instruments could only play a few different sounds, with jumps between them, something like this:

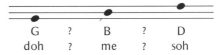

How can you tell by *looking* at these notes that there are jumps between the sounds? Which playing names have been jumped over, and which singing names?

But there was at least one more sound that could be made with instruments like horns and trumpets. This was another *soh*, a lower one, and if we want to write it we have to draw another line underneath the three we have already. While we are about it, we will draw yet another line at the top, making five altogether. We shall need all five lines very soon:

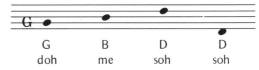

Now we have two notes with the same playing name (D) and the same singing name (*soh*). The new D is an *octave* below the old one.

6

How many sounds do you have to jump over if you go straight from high D to low D?

Here are some horn or trumpet signals to play or sing:

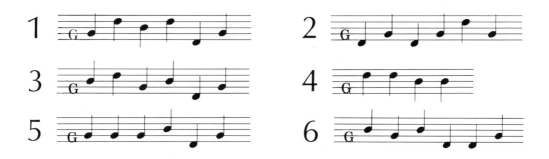

CLOCK CHIMES

The Westminster chimes, which ring out every quarter of an hour from the clock tower of the Houses of Parliament, are played on four bells arranged to make a different pattern at each quarter, like this:

The pattern grows longer at each quarter until the full hour is reached, when we hear all sixteen notes (but still only four different bells). 'Big Ben' then follows with his deeper sound, which he strikes from one to twelve times.

We have given the letter-names or 'playing names' of the four notes that make up the first quarter, and underneath are the solfa or 'singing names'. Play these notes on any instruments you have, and sing them also. For the other quarters you must of course arrange the letter and solfa names in different orders, but remember there are still only four of each.

Another bell tune comes from France. It moves along most of the time in regular crotchets, but there are four places in the tune where you can see a note with an empty head.

This is called a *minim*. When we play or sing a note like this we must go on feeling the regular crotchet beats but make only one sound lasting for two beats. It will help to keep the minims the right length if someone quietly taps the beats all through on a drum, tambourine, or triangle:

Bells are ring-ing loud and clear: Some are far off, some are near.

Triangle or other percussion   *(and so on)*

Some in clocks to   count the hours,   Some high up in   tall church towers.

Our third bell tune is very short, but we can make it into a longer piece if we sing or play it as a *round*. To do this we divide our class or group into three teams. Team 1 starts, and when it has played four notes Team 2 also starts from the beginning. Team 3 listens to Team 2, waits for it to play four notes, and then it is the time for Team 3 to start. Of course Teams 1 and 2 will get to the end first, but they can go straight back to the beginning and sing or play it all again. In fact it is quite a good idea for each of the three teams to play the whole tune three times over and then stop, each team dropping out in turn.

But before beginning at all we must learn to find an extra note called F sharp. It is quite easy to find on the recorder, using two hands. On the piano it is one of the black keys:

If you are using a glockenspiel or xylophone you will have to take out the F bar and put in one marked F sharp or F♯. If you are using singing names, the name for the extra sound is *te*.

THE LITTLE BELL AT WESTMINSTER

[and so on, until each team has sung through the song three times, and then dropped out. Team 3 finishes alone.]

Things to do

Draw five parallel lines with narrow spaces between them. This is called a stave. Make a small capital G across the second line up to remind you of the name of this line and help to name the others more easily.

Now get ready to spell out some words on the stave. Each word has three letters. Make crotchets for the first and second letters, but a minim for the third letter. Then each word will have the same time pattern, but the heads of the crotchets or minims will stand on different lines or in different spaces. Here is an example: what word do these notes spell?

? ? ?

We have put two upright lines across the stave after the 'word'. This is called a *double bar*, and is like a full stop in writing words. Make a double bar after each word you spell in notes.

Now try these:

G A G	B E G
D A D	C A D
A G E	A C E
G A B	A D D

When you have written the notes, play or sing them. You can make this into a game with a partner, one playing and the other saying what the word is.

THE G LADDER

If we take all the notes we have used so far, and add an E on the bottom line of the stave, we can make two ladders, a long one and a short one:

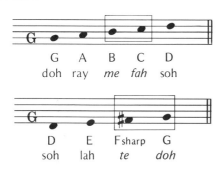

G	A	B	C	D
doh	ray	*me*	*fah*	soh

D	E	F sharp	G
soh	lah	*te*	*doh*

The long ladder has five notes and starts from the singing name *doh* (playing name G). You can play all five notes on the recorder with left hand fingers only. All five are white keys on the piano.

The short ladder has only four notes, with G at the top and the black F sharp just below it.

The rungs or steps of these ladders all look the same distance apart, but some of them are really closer together than the others. These are the rungs with the singing names *me-fah* and *te-doh*. Whenever these pairs of singing names come together they make small steps, called *semitones*. The other steps are all alike and are called *whole tones*.

One of the semitones is the step between B and C. Find these two notes on the piano. Both are white keys. They have no black key between them. Why?

If we like we can make one long ladder, like this:

E   F sharp   G

You can find these notes on the piano, but they are not quite so easy on the recorder, and you may not be able to reach the two highest with your voices.

13

Whenever *doh* is G we are sure to keep wanting F sharp instead of F. So to save time and trouble we hoist a sharp on to the top line of the stave, as a warning signal that *doh* is going to be G, and any note on the top line or in the bottom space is F sharp:

— Now F sharp.

—F sharp here too.

The G sign we have been putting on the second line of the stave is usually written and printed in an ornamental curly shape like this:

We will use this form of the G or *treble clef* in future.

WE ARE THE MUSIC MAKERS

soh   doh
We   are   the   mu - sic   ma - kers   who   tra - vel   round   the

land.   We   are   the   mu - sic   ma - kers   who   tra - vel round the

Things to do

1 The song 'We are the music makers' comes from a part of Czechoslovakia called Moravia. Look for it on a map. The words mention several instruments. Try to find pictures of them.

2 Learn to write the new signs. A sharp is made of two small upright strokes with two slanting strokes across them. When it is put on the stave, the line or space must show through the middle of the sign. Although we say 'F sharp' what we write is really 'sharp F'.

　The G or treble clef is a beautiful spiral, and we start making it on the second line of the stave and continue without lifting the pencil from the paper.

3 There are two more new signs in 'We are the music makers'. They mark silences or rests. When you see a crotchet rest like this ♪ or like this ⅃ count one beat but do not sing or play any sound. The small black mark lying on a line of the stave is a minim rest, and tells you to keep silent while counting two beats:

4 Feel and count your pulse with the tips of your fingers against the other wrist, on the thumb side. Most young peoples' pulses beat about 80 times a minute, but the rate gets quicker when they run or are excited. Listen to a watch ticking. Is it quicker or slower than your pulse?

5 Here is another tune from Moravia to play on the recorder or other melodic instrument. It is a lullaby with only three different notes in it. Underneath is another tune, of four notes, which will fit the lullaby if both players count their beats at the same rate:

First player

Second player

[Remember—The bottom space is F sharp!]

The curved lines mean play smoothly, and only take breath at the end of a curve. The dot after the last minim for the second player means that this note is to be held for three beats. We call this a *dotted minim.* There is another at the end of 'We are the music makers'.

PATTERNS OF BEATS

When we feel a pulse, or listen to a clock or watch ticking, after a little while the beats seem to make a pattern, although they are really all alike. In our minds they make a pattern of *twos*:

1 2   1 2

or a pattern of *threes*:

1 2 3   1 2 3

or a pattern of *fours*:

1 2 3 4   1 2 3 4

These are the most usual patterns we seem to hear, but if we try we can imagine others.

In music these patterns are *not* imaginary. The first beat of a group of twos, threes, fours and so on actually is a little stronger than the others. We show the stronger beats when we write music by putting small upright strokes through the stave just before them. The strokes are called *bar-lines*, and the notes between one bar-line and the next make up a bar of music.

But the music does not always begin with a strong beat. Often the first note we hear or sing or play is on one of the weaker beats, so that the pattern is more like this:

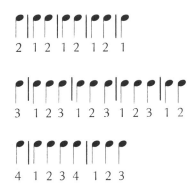

2 1 2 1 2 1 2 1

3 1 2 3   1 2 3   1 2 3   1 2

4 1 2 3 4   1 2 3

If you look at the songs in this book, you can see that many of them start with one of these *up-beats*, as they are called.

Another thing we do to make the pattern clear is to put a special sign, or time-signature, on the stave right at the beginning of the music. There are several ways of doing this, but the sort of time-signature we will use for the present is $\frac{2}{}$ To show there will be two beats in every bar

$\frac{3}{}$ for patterns of three beats

$\frac{4}{}$ for patterns of four beats.

Here are two songs to sing. One has a pulse-pattern of threes, the other of fours. One starts on an up-beat, the other on a down-beat.

THE BUSY FARMER

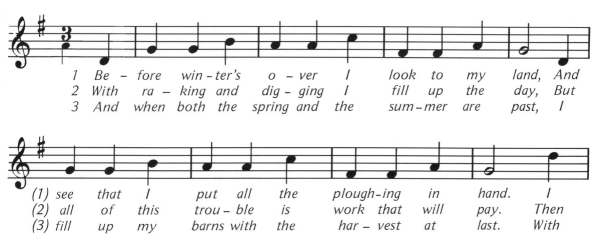

1 Be - fore win - ter's o - ver I look to my land, And
2 With ra - king and dig - ging I fill up the day, But
3 And when both the spring and the sum - mer are past, I

(1) see that I put all the plough-ing in hand. I
(2) all of this trou - ble is work that will pay. Then
(3) fill up my barns with the har - vest at last. With

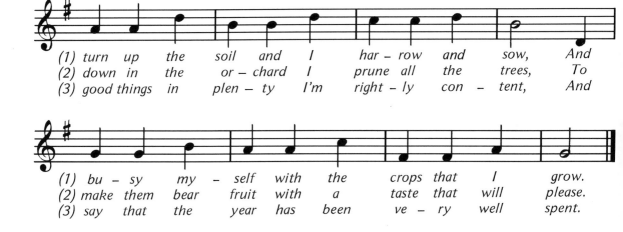

(1) turn up the soil and I har - row and sow, And
(2) down in the or - chard I prune all the trees, To
(3) good things in plen - ty I'm right - ly con - tent, And

(1) bu - sy my - self with the crops that I grow.
(2) make them bear fruit with a taste that will please.
(3) say that the year has been ve - ry well spent.

SHEEP-SHEARING DAY

LONGS AND SHORTS

In 1844 an American named Samuel Morse sent the first electric telegraph message between two towns. He invented a set of signals for all the letters of the alphabet, made up of long and short buzzes, or long and short flashes of light. These are called the *Morse Code*.

Here are some of the 'dashes' and 'dots' for a few letters of the Code:

D — •• (long and 2 shorts)

M — — (2 longs)

H •••• (4 shorts)

U •• — (2 shorts and a long)

Beside each letter you can see the longs and shorts written in musical notes. The long or 'dash' is like a crotchet or one-beat note. Two shorts or 'dots' are a pair of *quavers* or half-beats like this:

Sometimes we need to write one quaver on its own, with a small slanting tail fixed to its stem ♪ , but when the quavers come as a pair they are usually fastened together by their tails.

Here is a little song from France, which you can sing either in English or French. There are only two different notes, A and G (*ray* and *doh*) until near the end, when the tune flies up to C and D (*fah* and *soh*):

23

THERE'S A CHICKEN ON A WALL

There's a chic-ken on a wall, Ea-ting all the crumbs that
U-ne pou-le sur un mur, Qui pi-co-tait du pain

fall: Pec-king here, pec-king there, Till she flies up in the air.
dur: Pi-co-ti, pi-co-ta, Lèv' la queue et puis s'en va.

Most people know the old street cry 'Hot cross buns', but may not have tried it as a round. Here it is, with some help in singing or playing it. The 'leader' starts the song, and the 'follower' joins in with the same tune just one bar later. Of course the 'follower' finishes last. The small blocks hanging from the middle line of the stave are *whole-bar rests*. We have printed a few of the singing names. The key-signature of one sharp is not absolutely necessary for this tune — why not?

HOT CROSS BUNS

The sad song about the wolf and the sheep comes from France. Although it is quite long, there are only five notes of the G ladder in the tune.

THE WOLF AND
THE SHEPHERD BOY

1 My ___ fa-ther's a far-mer And I ten-ded his sheep, So I
2 There ___ weren't ma-ny of them, And I watched them all day, But a
3 The ___ wolf went on eat-ing, Un-til he was full, And ___
4 I ___ carved out a flute from a ___ bone that I found, And ___

(1) went to the pas-ture, a good watch to keep. To
(2) wolf came and caught one and dragged it a - way. A -
(3) when he ran off he left on - ly the wool. The
(4) now my poor sheep makes a sor - row - ful sound. A

26

(1) keep, to keep, There weren't ma – ny of them, To
(2) – way, a – way, A wolf came and caught one, A –
(3) wool, the wool, And that's all he left me, The
(4) sound, a sound, My poor sheep is ma – king, A

(1) keep, to keep, A good watch to keep.
(2) – way, a – way, He dragged it a – way.
(3) wool, the wool, He left me the wool.
(4) sound, a sound, A sor – row – ful sound.

Things to do

1 Find out more about the Morse Code. Later on we shall borrow other signs from it to help with the musical ones. Just for the present try writing two more letters from the Morse Code as musical notes, using crotchets and pairs of quavers. These are:

X   — •• —

Z   — — ••

2 Practise making quavers on paper.
For a single quaver begin with the head: ●

Then fit on the stem:

Lastly put on the small slanting tail: ♪

Then try it the other way up: 𝄆

For a pair of quavers, make the two heads (not too close to each other): ● ●

Then add their stems: ♩ ♩

Lastly put on the tail joining the stems: ♫

Then try it the other way up: 𝆕

CHANGING THE KEY-NOTE

Up to now all our tunes have had G as *doh*. But any sound can be *doh*, and it is sometimes good to have a change. Suppose we decide that D is to be *doh*, and make a fresh ladder or scale. There will have to be an F sharp again, to make the semitone between *me* and *fah*. And then right at the top we shall have to use a new note, C sharp, to make the semitone between *te* and *doh*:

D	E	Fsharp	G	A	B	Csharp	D
doh	*ray*	*me*	*fah*	*soh*	*lah*	*te*	*doh*

To save writing C sharp every time we want it, we put it into the key signature along with the F sharp we had before:

Whenever we see this two-sharp signature, we know that D is going to be *doh*.

C sharp is another of the black keys on the piano, and it has a special (and very easy) fingering on the recorder.

Here is a song written in the key of D. It comes from Poland, and tells of a hare that got the better of the hunters:

THE HARE THAT GOT AWAY

1 Once a lit – tle hare sat on the grass,
2 Now the hare in ter – ror hears the horn,
3 There's no time for him to say good – day,
4 Till he rea – ches safe – ty in the wood,

(1) on the grass, Thought he'd wait and let the hun – ters
(2) hears the horn, Straight a – way he's up and in the
(3) say good – day, And he does – n't have to ask the
(4) in the wood, Ly – ing in the grass now he feels

(1) pass, hun – ters ____ pass. But the hun – ters soon were round him,
(2) corn, in the ____ corn. Pan – ting he runs through the clo – ver,
(3) way, ask the ____ way. Though he's wear – y, on he ru – shes,
(4) good, he feels ____ good. In the mud the dogs are slip – ping,

(1) Sure e – nough their dogs had found him: Run, hare, run! Run, hare, run!
(2) But the dan – ger's still not o – ver: He's in view! He's in view!
(3) O – ver fur – rows, un – der bu – shes, Like the wind! Like the wind!
(4) Head to foot the men are drip – ping, Home they go! Home they go!

'Fire in the mountains' is an old ring game. The inside circle sits or kneels on the floor. The outside circle, which must have one extra person, moves round. The inside circle sings, but stops suddenly at an agreed moment. The outside circle must try to find partners, and the player left over must then change places with someone from the inside circle.

FIRE IN THE MOUNTAINS

Fire in the moun - tains, Run, boys, run,

You with the red coat, fol-low with the gun, Drums will beat and

you will run, Fire in the moun - tains, Run, — boys, — run.

'Black Monday' used to be a favourite song for blacksmiths' apprentices to sing as they hammered away in the iron-working districts of Austria. As the midday meal was part of their wages they naturally took a great deal of interest in what there was for dinner.

BLACK MONDAY

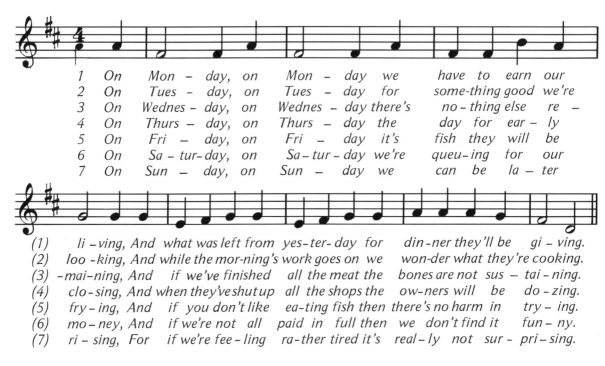

Things to do

1 Find on maps the foreign countries some of our songs have come from. They include France, Germany, Austria, Czechoslovakia, and Poland.

2 Make sure of the D scale on any instruments you have. It is a very good scale for the descant recorder, because you can play all of its eight notes without 'overblowing'. On the piano you will need to use two black keys, and for tuned percussion you will need extra F sharp and C sharp bars or tubes. D is the best of all keys for the violin.

3 Set out the chime bars, glockenspiel, or xylophone ready to play the D scale, with an extra E at the top if possible. Then take a beater in each hand and try a kind of leapfrog exercise, like this (L stands for left hand, R for right):

If you add a *low* C sharp to the scale, you
can leapfrog downwards:

(extra C sharp)

R L   R L   R

These leapfrog jumps, missing out a step
of the scale every time, are called *thirds*.

Now use both beaters together so that the
thirds sound at the same time, making a
chain:

You can try all these exercises on the
piano, using the forefinger of each hand.

4 Make up some drum rhythms to go with
'Fire in the mountains'. Here are a few
examples:

Invent others, and try changing from one
pattern to another during the song. You
can use other percussion instruments too,
and make the piece longer by going
through the tune several times.

5 Can you find other rhymes or songs like
'Black Monday', which mention all the
days of the week?

36

THE WISE FOOLS OF GOTHAM

Gotham is a village a few miles away from the town of Nottingham. Long ago, in the reign of King John, the people of Gotham heard that the King was on his way to Nottingham and intended to pass through the village. They did not like this news at all, for someone had told them that any land the King walked or rode over at once became royal land. Their fields, their houses, their animals, and their crops would then belong to the King.

The people wondered how they could prevent King John from coming near their village. At last they agreed upon a plan. They would all pretend to be as stupid as possible, so that the King and his courtiers would not want to have anything to do with them.

Just as they expected, some of the King's men arrived one evening to tell them that he was near, and they were all to turn out in their best clothes to welcome him. One of

the men blew a trumpet and another beat a drum to attract attention and make the simple villagers believe that this was a very special occasion. But when the King's messengers reached the village they began to see strange things.

First, they saw a group of men and women hard at work making a kind of cage out of green branches, while the children were trying to catch a bird that fluttered around. Everyone was singing, but a few broke off their song to explain that they wanted to build a hedge round the cuckoo so that she could not fly away. Whenever the cuckoo left them it was always a sign that summer was over, so they thought that if they could somehow keep her in Gotham they might have lovely summer weather all the year round.

The King's men looked at each other, shook their heads, and went on a little further. Soon they saw a big round cheese rolling by, and then another and another. At the top of a small hill they found a group of people pushing yellow cheeses downhill as if they were cart wheels. When asked why they were doing this, they explained that they thought it was the quickest way to send the cheeses to be sold in Nottingham market.

The messengers again shook their heads. By this time it was getting dark and the moon had risen. In the middle of the village was a pond, and round it stood men and boys with fishing rods and nets. They were pointing to the middle of the pond, where the full moon was reflected in the water. "Look", they said "there is another moon, floating in the pond. If we can fish it out we shall have two moons instead of one, and our village will be better lit at night."

After hearing this, the messengers shrugged their shoulders and decided to give up. They agreed that the King could not possibly come to a village where all the people were mad, and they went back and advised their royal master to go to Nottingham by a different road. So the wise fools of Gotham had their own way after all.

MAKING MUSIC FOR THE STORY

1 *Music for the King's messengers* Make up a trumpet signal from these four notes:

You can play them in any order, and turn them into crotchets or quavers or a mixture of both. Use recorders, or melodicas if you have any — they sound quite trumpet-like. Make up some drum patterns too.

2 *The Gotham cuckoo round* This very old song is a round for three groups of singers. It also makes a good piece for recorders or other instruments. Group 1 starts the song, group 2 waits until group 1 has finished the first line of the music and then starts from the beginning, and group 3 starts last of all. Each group can sing the round through several times.

THE GOTHAM CUCKOO

3 *Rolling the cheeses* One way of making this into a sound-picture is to use drums of different sizes, with soft-headed sticks. The drum-strokes can suggest the rolling and bumping as the cheeses go down the hill. What will happen to the speed of the strokes as the rolling goes on? Will the sounds grow louder or softer as the cheeses continue their journey?

Another way of making the sound-picture is to invent a rolling tune that starts at the top of the scale and goes step by step down to the bottom. Here is an example, written in two lines so that it can be played like a round, using recorders or tuned percussion:

When 'leaders' and 'followers' are playing together they make a chain of *thirds*. The piece can be played through more than once. On arriving at the bottom of the scale the 'leaders' count two crotchet beats' silence, then three more (a whole-bar rest), and then start from the beginning again. The 'followers' play a D to finish their scale, count two beats' silence, then three more, and start again.

The real moon and the moon's reflection in the water

Here is a smooth tune for the real moon shining down from the sky:

And this is the same tune turned upside down, for the moon's reflection in the water:

When you can play both of them separately, try putting them together. This piece can be played several times over without stopping. Do not hurry, and be sure to count an exact 'one — two' for every minim.

The end of the story
Make up some more trumpet and drum music for the King's messengers as they leave the village, with the sounds dying away as they get further off.

Things to do

1 You can put the story and the music together, turning it either into a play or into a mime without spoken words.

2 You can make a set of pictures in the form of a strip cartoon or a wall-frieze to illustrate the story.

3 Here are some rhymes that have been written about the wise fools, imagining them setting out into the open sea. You could try illustrating these also, or perhaps even make up music for them:

(i) *Three wise men of Gotham*
went to sea in a bowl.
If the bowl had been stronger,
my tale had been longer.

40

(ii)　*In a bowl to sea went wise men three,*
　　　On a brilliant night in June;
　　They carried a net, and their hearts were set
　　　On fishing up the moon.

　　The sea was calm, the air was balm,
　　　Not a breath stirred low or high,
　　And the moon, I trow, lay as bright below,
　　　And round as in the sky.

　　The wise men with the current went,
　　　Nor paddle nor oar had they,
　　And still as the grave they went on the wave,
　　　That they might not disturb their prey.

　　Far, far at sea were the wise men three,
　　　When their fishing-net they threw;
　　And at the throw, the moon below
　　　In a thousand fragments flew.

　　The sea was bright with dancing light
　　　Of a million million gleams,
　　Which the broken moon shot forth as soon
　　　As the net disturbed her beams.

　　They drew in their net: it was empty and wet,
　　　And they had lost their pain;
　　Soon ceased the play of each dancing ray,
　　　And the image was round again.

　　Three times they threw, three times they drew,
　　　And all the while were mute;
　　And evermore their wonder grew,
　　　Till they could not but dispute.

　　Their silence they broke, and each one spoke
　　　Full long, and loud, and clear;
　　A man at sea their voices three
　　　Full three leagues off might hear.

The three wise men got home again
  To their children and their wives;
But, touching their trip, and their net's vain dip,
  They disputed all their lives.

The wise men three could never agree
  Why they missed the promised boon.
They agreed alone that their net they had thrown,
  And they had not caught the moon.

4 This Dutch round is about the way the cuckoo changes her tune as the summer goes on. It is more difficult than the Gotham round because of the leaps in the tune, which start with a *third* and get gradually wider — a *fourth*, a *fifth*, a *sixth*, a *seventh*, and finally an *octave*:

IN MAY WE HEAR THE CUCKOO SING

1 In   May we hear the   cuc-koo sing, and then she calls 'Cuc-koo!'

2 She   chan-ges la-ter   in the year, and then her voice is   not so clear:

3 'Cuc-koo! cuc-koo! cuc-koo! cuc-koo! cuc-koo! cuc-koo!cuc-koo!'

SOME EXPERIMENTS WITH SOUNDS

Experiment 1 Hold about 5 centimetres of an ordinary flat ruler firmly on a table near the edge, and use your other hand to twang the part of the ruler that is hanging over. You will see the ruler vibrate, and you will hear a sound: it may be just a buzz, or it may be something like a musical sound. This sound is caused by the vibrating wood pushing the air round it backwards and forwards and so making invisible waves in the air. Our ears catch the air-waves and send them to a part of the brain which recognises them as sounds — high or low, loud or soft.

Experiment 2 Throw a small stone into the middle of a pool or bowl of water and watch the ripples spread out. The stone has disturbed the water all round it, making a wave, and this in its turn starts a whole series of waves spreading from the centre of the pool or bowl to its edge. These water-waves can be seen, but air-waves are invisible.

Experiment 3 Hold one end of a skipping-rope and lay the rest straight out along the ground. Shake the end you are holding, and waves will travel along the rope. Each bit of the rope passes on its wave-movement to the next, but the rope stays where you laid it on the ground.

Experiment 4 Take the ruler again, and hold a slightly longer piece firmly on the table, so that there is less of it hanging over the edge. Twang it again. Do you notice any difference in the sound? Do you notice any change in the look of the vibrating wood? Try the same experiment several times, with different lengths of wood hanging over.

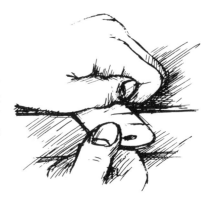

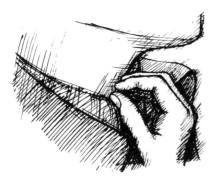

Experiment 5 Hold the finger-tips of one hand lightly against your throat, close to the 'Adam's apple', and hum (*m-m-m-m*) fairly loudly. What do you feel? Now do the same thing again, but this time keep your teeth apart and your lips lightly together. You will probably feel your lips vibrating, and perhaps other parts of your face too.

Experiment 6 Tie one end of a piece of fairly thin but smooth string, or a piece of thin wire, about one metre in length, to a hook in the wall or other firm support. Fasten to the other end a weight such as an ordinary brick, and hang the weight over a chair-back about the same height as the hook. Let the weight hang quite free so that it stretches the string tight. Twang the string to make a musical sound. Now move the chair a little nearer the wall, and twang again. What has happened to the sound?

Experiment 7 Keep the chair in the same position, but tie on more weight. This will make the string tighter, or as we say, increase the *tension*. What happens to the sound this time?

Experiment 8 Hold a strong elastic band stretched out in the air between your hands, or between two rulers. Ask someone to twang the elastic. Then try stretching the same elastic band over a small wooden box or drawer, and listen to it again. Which sound do you think is clearer and stronger? Can you explain the difference?

Experiment 9 Use a box similar to the one in Experiment 8, and stretch across it two elastic bands of the same length but different thickness. Compare their sounds.

What these experiments have shown

Copy these sentences and fill in each blank space with a suitable word:

1 A sound is caused when something _____ and makes waves in the _____.

2 Rapid vibrations make ____ sounds than slow ones.

3 The more a string is stretched, the ____ it sounds.

4 A thicker string makes a _____ sound than a thinner one, if both are the same length and have the same tension.

5 If a stretched string is twanged hard, it makes a _____ sound than if it is twanged gently, because the string moves further backwards and forwards. But the sound does not get _____ or _____.

6 A sound that is faint to begin with becomes _____ if we let it pass on its vibrations to a box or table.

HONEY BEES

To begin with, here is a very easy song about the bee.
(Remember to count through the crotchet rests.)

SUM, SUM, SUM

[Before verse 1]

Sum, sum, sum, That's the bee's loud hum.

[Begin each verse here]

1 *Up and down the wor-ker pas-ses, Fly-ing o – ver flowers and gras-ses:*
2 *In the field and in the gar-den Ga-ther nec-tar, ga-ther pol-len:*
3 *Then fly back with bur-den hea-vy To the bee-hive, full and bu-sy:*

[Sing this after each verse]

Sum, sum, sum, That's the bee's loud hum.

Of the many kinds of bees in the world, those most useful to man are the honey or hive bees. They live in colonies, usually in the hives or skeps placed ready for them by bee-keepers. Each colony has one queen bee, who is the largest and most important member of it and can lay two to three thousand eggs in a day. The rest of the colony is made up of several hundred drones or male bees, and many thousands of workers, which collect nectar and pollen from flowers, make honey and 'bee-bread' to feed the whole colony, make wax for the cells or combs, feed the grubs, chase out intruders, and keep the hive clean and cool. The worker bees even have a kind of dance to show one another where the best nectar can be found in gardens, fields and hedges.

From time to time one of the grubs that hatch out of the eggs is specially fed and looked after to become a queen bee. But there cannot be more than one queen reigning in a hive, and so either the old queen or the new one flies off, followed by a large number of workers and drones, to find another home. This is called swarming. If the bee-keeper sees that swarming is going on he attracts the homeless queen into an empty hive, where the rest of the swarm will follow her, make new wax cells, and start a fresh colony.

Queen bees and workers are armed with stings to defend the hive, but they do not usually attack human beings unless they are disturbed.

Country people used to believe that a swarm could be made to settle by banging metal pans and other noisy objects. There may be some truth in this. Bees have no sense of hearing, but they can probably feel vibrations in some way. A song that has come down to us from the days of the first Queen Elizabeth refers to this belief. It can be sung as a round, with as many as four groups joining in:

BEE ROUND

1. *Bring out your ket - tle of*

2. *pur - est me - tal to*

3. *set - tle, to set - tle the*

4. *swarm of bees.*

49

Another song about swarming bees comes from Latvia, on the Baltic Sea. It belongs to the days when every peasant liked to have a hive of bees in his garden, and if he found a swarm in the woods he could capture and keep it, on condition he paid a tax to the bee-ward, an official employed by the local land-owner.

THE BEE-SWARM

1 Down the ri – ver floats a tree branch
2 Sad – ly there be – side the ri – ver
3 'If we lose you, bees so pre – cious,
4 'You with – out the wood – land flow – ers

(1) All with ho – ney – bees a – swar – ming, Down the ri – ver
(2) Stands the bee – ward's bride a – wee – ping, Sad – ly there be –
(3) All our sum – mer joys will pe – rish, If we lose you,
(4) Could not ga – ther your sweet nec – tar, So are we, dear

(1) floats a tree branch, All with ho – ney – bees a – swarm.
(2) – side the ri – ver, Stands the bee – ward's bride and weeps.
(3) bees so pre – cious, All our sum – mer joys will die.'
(4) bees, with – out you, Sad and drear the sum – mer through.'

Things to do

1 Find out more about the lives of bees. One thing we have already learnt is that they cannot hear in the same way as man and animals do, nor have they any voices. They make their buzzing sound by moving their wings very rapidly as they fly or hover.

2 What shape are the wax cells in a beehive? Learn more about this shape, and where else it can be found in nature.

3 Collect sayings, rhymes, and stories about bees. In the Bible there is a strange story about Samson, the strong man, and his riddle that no one could solve. Part of the riddle was: 'Out of the strong came forth sweetness'. The story, with the answer, is in the Book of Judges, Chapter 14.

Here are some bee-rhymes to start your collection:

1) Little bird of paradise,
 she works her work both neat and nice;
 she pleases God, she pleases man,
 she does the work that no man can.

2) If bees stay home, rain will soon come.
 If bees fly away, it will be a fine day.

3) A swarm of bees in May
  is worth a load of hay.
 A swarm of bees in June
  is worth a silver spoon.
 A swarm of bees in July
  is not worth a fly.

4) *How merrily looks the man that hath gold;*
      he seemeth but twenty, though three score years old.
   How nimble the bee that flieth about
      and gathereth honey within and without.
   But men without money, and bees without honey,
      are nothing better than drones.

4 If you have piano lessons, you can find in a book called
   The Show-booth for Bold Pianists an interesting puzzle-
   piece by a Polish composer. It has the title 'An obstinate
   little bee', and can be put together in a different way each
   time you play it.

A SCALE WITHOUT SHARPS

So far we have used two scales, G and D. We chose them because they are easy to play on most instruments and comfortable to sing. We learnt that these two scales need sharps to make the semitones between *me* and *fah* and *te* and *doh*.

It is possible to make a scale that does not need any sharps. This is the scale that has C as *doh*. It is not very easy to play on the descant recorder, but it is the easiest of all scales to find and remember on the piano, as every step can be played with a white key — no black ones need be touched. And if you are using a xylophone or glockenspiel you will not have to change any of the wooden or metal bars.

Start on C on the piano and go steadily up to the next C, all on the white keys and not missing any out. On the way you will touch E and F; they make the *me – fah* semitone. At the top of the scale you will play B and C, which give the *te – doh* semitone. These two pairs of keys have no black key between them, because they make sounds that are only a semitone apart. The piano is a scale-of-C instrument. All other scales on the keyboard need at least one black key to make them sound right.

Writing the scale of C has one problem we must solve before we go any further. If we start it from the top and go downwards we soon realise what the problem is:

C	B	A	G	F	E	D	C
doh	te	lah	soh	fah	me	ray	doh

We need one more note to finish the scale on bottom C (*doh*), but we have run out of lines on the stave. The only thing to do is to put in a small bit of extra line specially for this C. This is called a *leger line*:

C
doh

Hundreds of years ago, before singers had keyboard instruments like the piano to help them, the semitones used to give a lot of trouble, until an ingenious choirmaster named Guido (Guy) thought of fitting to the scale a set of syllables or 'singing names' very much like the 'solfa' we still use. Then the choir could practise going up and down the six-note ladder with the help of the 'singing names', making sure to sing a semitone between *me* and *fah*. When they had got this right, they would sometimes turn the ladder into a little prayer to St Nicholas, the patron saint of choristers:

doh ray me fah soh lah, lah soh fah me ray doh.
Help me, Saint Ni - cho - las, help me to sing in tune.

Here is another song made out of the same six notes (or *hexachord*). It used to be sung in Germany by children who went round the streets after dark, carrying home-made lanterns:

MY LANTERN

lah soh me   soh me doh
My lan - tern, my lan - tern,   Sun and moon and star - light, You can

shine up there, You can shine down here, But you don't have to put out my   lan - tern clear.

TWO RAIN SPELLS

The next song has only three different notes in it. It is an old magic song they used to sing in Russia, when the fields were dry and needed rain:

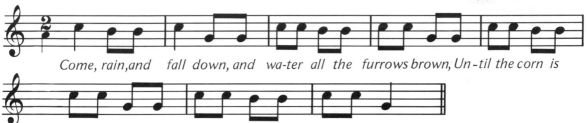

Come, rain, and fall down, and wa-ter all the furrows brown, Un-til the corn is fresh and green, and flies and gnats no more are seen.

There is a little English song which tries to do the opposite of the Russian one — it tells the rain to stop. We would have printed this one also without a key-signature, but decided to use G as *doh* instead. C would have made it awkward to sing. Can you think why?

Rain, rain, go to Spain and ne-ver-more come back a-gain.

For our last song, however, we go back to the C scale, but without using the leger-line C at all. The song is from Czecho-slovakia, and has a dance rhythm like a waltz:

SHEPHERD'S DANCE SONG

Sheep go wan – de – ring deep in the fo – rest, And
all through the clea – rings they feed and they roam.
I call them: 'Don't go in too far!' They an – swer:
'Baa,— baa,— baa!' Come back, sheep, for it's time we went home.

Things to do

1 Find out more about Saint Nicholas. He looked after choir singers, travellers, and children, and we also know him as Santa Claus.

2 The hexachord or scale of six notes can be arranged in 1 x 2 x 3 x 4 x 5 x 6 different ways. If you can work out this sum the answer will surprise you.

3 Practise writing C on a leger line below the five-line stave. Make the leger line short, thin, and the same distance below the stave as all the main lines are apart. Then put the head of a crotchet across the leger line, and add the stem pointing upwards. Practise writing D also. This note hangs from the bottom main line:

C   D

56

A USEFUL TIME-PATTERN

Work in pairs, or in two equal-size groups, **A and B.**
Both groups count aloud steadily: *one, two, one, two* **and**
then begin to clap.

Group A claps crotchets

Group B claps a crotchet and
two quavers

When you are sure you can keep these two patterns going
together, try this:

Group A still claps crotchets

Group B claps the crotchet but only
thinks the first of the two quavers

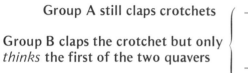

(But Group B will still *hear* A's crotchet sounding on the
'*think*' quaver.)

Now change over, so that Group B has the steady crotchets,
while Group A has the *crotchet — (think) — quaver* pattern.

Group A

Group B

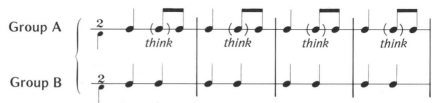

Now both Groups can try the new *crotchet — (think) —
quaver* pattern, clapping together. This is really hard, because there will no longer be the sound of the second crotchet
in the background.

There is a neat way of writing this new pattern. We write a crotchet, and after it a dot (to take the place of the missing quaver), and lastly the single quaver:

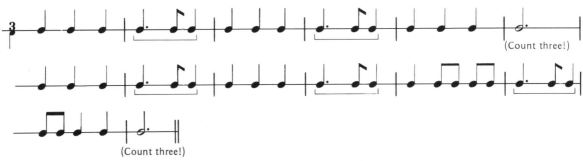

Now try this, and see if you can recognise a familiar tune from its time-pattern:

(Count three!)

(Count three!)

This time-pattern, *dotted crotchet — quaver*, occurs in hundreds of tunes. Here are a few to sing or play; the first two are rounds:

TURN AGAIN, WHITTINGTON

1 Turn a-gain Whittington,

2 thou worthy ci – ti-zen,

3 Lord Mayor of London.

58

HORSE-RIDING

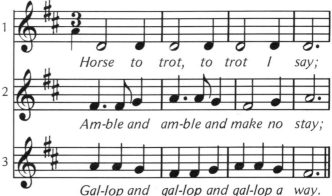

1. Horse to trot, to trot I say;

2. Am-ble and am-ble and make no stay;

3. Gal-lop and gal-lop and gal-lop a way.

The next two songs have interesting shapes. We know already that the long curves or *slurs* over the notes remind us to try to sing or play each group of notes in one breath. They also show how many bars make up a phrase. In 'Bird of Beauty' the first phrase is four bars long, and so is the second. But what about the third and fourth phrases? In 'Wedding Dance' the first and second phrases are both three bars long. What about the third and fourth phrases?

BIRD OF BEAUTY

1 Bird of beau-ty, I a-dore__ you, All my life I've

2 Bird of beau-ty, Can you doubt__ me? Do you think I'll

(1) wai – ted for__ you; I have kept you al – ways in sight,

(2) live with-out __ you? Can you go a – way and leave me,

(1)Thought of you by day and by night.

(2) As the ap – ple falls from the tree?

WEDDING DANCE

1 Look, they said, the old man's fi - nished,
2 We will have a jol - ly wed - ding

(1) But you see I'm fit and spry. There's still time for
(2) When I've found a lov - ing wife. There'll be mus - ic

(1) me to mar - ry, A - ny - way, I'm going to try.
(2) there'll be dan - cing, No - thing like en - joy - ing life.

JOHN BARLEYCORN

This fine old English country song tells the whole story of the sowing of seed, its growth, its harvesting, and its preparation for food and drink. The story of the seed is told as if it were a living person, who was buried, apparently died, came to life again, and then suffered more ill-treatment. All the processes, including ploughing, harrowing, sowing, harvesting, and threshing, were carried out by hand in the days when the song grew up. Now machines make the work easier, but the seed still has to be left to grow and ripen.

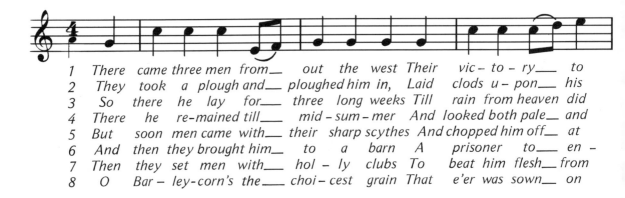

1 There came three men from__ out the west Their vic – to – ry__ to
2 They took a plough and__ ploughed him in, Laid clods u – pon__ his
3 So there he lay for__ three long weeks Till rain from heaven did
4 There he re-mained till__ mid – sum – mer And looked both pale__ and
5 But soon men came with__ their sharp scythes And chopped him off__ at
6 And then they brought him__ to a barn A prisoner to__ en –
7 Then they set men with__ hol – ly clubs To beat him flesh__ from
8 O Bar – ley-corn's the__ choi – cest grain That e'er was sown__ on

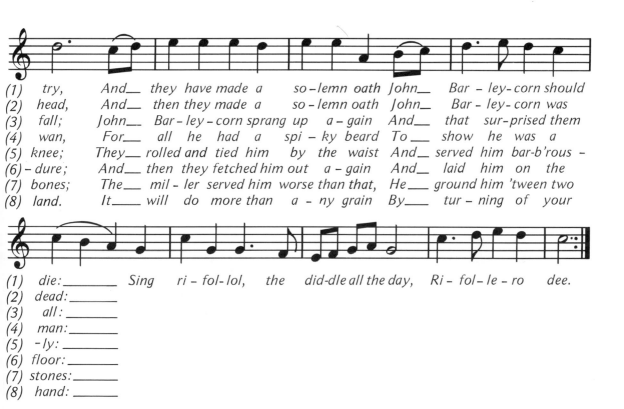

(1) try,	And— they have made a	so–lemn oath John—	Bar - ley-corn should
(2) head,	And— then they made a	so–lemn oath John—	Bar - ley- corn was
(3) fall;	John— Bar - ley - corn sprang up a – gain	And— that sur-prised them
(4) wan,	For— all he had a	spi – ky beard To —	show he was a
(5) knee;	They— rolled and tied him	by the waist And—	served him bar-b'rous -
(6) –dure;	And— then they fetched him out a – gain	And— laid him on the
(7) bones;	The— mil - ler served him worse than that,	He— ground him 'tween two
(8) land.	It— will do more than a - ny grain	By— tur - ning of your

(1) die: _____ Sing ri – fol-lol, the did-dle all the day, Ri - fol-le - ro dee.
(2) dead: _____
(3) all: _____
(4) man: _____
(5) -ly: _____
(6) floor: _____
(7) stones: _____
(8) hand: _____

Things to do

1 Practise writing the dotted crotchet — quaver pattern: ♩. ♪ Keep the dot small and not too far away from the crotchet-head.

2 Make up a mime to the story of John Barleycorn, or a set of pictures to illustrate it.

A field of barley

Photo: Jane Bown
Reproduced by permission of the Camera Press

3 Here is an old Irish hymn-tune that has lost its words. Play it on recorders or other instruments, and then see if you can make up some words to fit. The line marked 'accompaniment' is for another instrument to act as partner.

HYMN-TUNE
FROM FRESHFORD (IRELAND)

Accompaniment